FIVERR: 35 SERVICES FOR YOU TO SELL ON FIVERR

SERVICES FOR YOU TO SELL ON FIVERR

-Michael Ingram

10/1/2016

In this book I will show you thirty-five ways other people are making great money on Fiverr. If you can create similar gigs you could be making money too. Take action today

Fiverr: thirty-five different services for you to sell on Fiverr'

By Michael Ingram

Copyright 2016 Michael Ingram

This e book is licensed for your personal enjoyment only. It may not be re-sold or, given away to other people. If you would like to share this book with another Person, please purchase an additional copy for each recipient. If you're reading this and did not purchase it, or it was not purchased for your use only, please purchase your own copy from Amazon.com. Thank you for respecting the hard work of this Author.

This book is dedicated to my wonderful Family, both past and present, who have made me into who I've become today. I thank you for your patience and resilience. For those that supported me and those that didn't-thank you. This life has a steep learning curve and I have taken all of my high and low points and hopefully, grown as a result.

Before we start delving into the World of selling on Fiverr and lots of secret tricks, hacks and hints to get you ahead of the 'pack', I would like to genuinely thank you from the bottom of my heart for choosing my book. There are other books on similar subjects out there and I'm really grateful you've chosen this book above the others. My aim is a simple one and that's to give you great content and value for money.

When you've taken all you want from this book (statistically most people never read a book from cover to cover) it would be really helpful to me if you could leave a few positive words in a review on Amazon. I'm like most people and appreciate approval and encouragement to keep me following my dreams to be productive as an Author. Also, your positive feedback will help ensure others buy my books and hopefully help me earn a living (it's not as easy as it looks to produce a book).

Here is the link to review my book:

I thank you once again for your custom and generosity. If you want more information on me or the other books, or, courses I have published, please visit my Website:-

www.bonusincomegenerator.com

Earnings Disclaimer

Every effort has been made to accurately represent these products and their potential. Even though this industry is one of the few where one can write their own check in terms of earnings, there is no guarantee that you will earn any money using the techniques and ideas in these materials. Examples in these materials are not to be interpreted as a promise or guarantee of earnings. Earning potential is entirely dependent on the person using our product, ideas, techniques and the effort put forth. We do not purport this as a "get rich scheme." Your level of success in attaining the results claimed in our materials depends on the time you devote to the program, ideas techniques, knowledge and various skills. Since these factors differ according to individuals, we cannot guarantee your success or income level.

Materials in our product and our website may contain information that includes or is based upon forward-looking statements within the meaning of the securities litigation reform act of 1995. Forward-looking statements give our expectations or forecasts of future events. You can identify these statements by the fact that they do not relate strictly to historical or current facts. They use words such as "anticipate," "estimate," "expect," "project," "intend," "believe," "plan," and other words and terms of similar meaning in connection with a description of potential earnings or financial performance. Any and all forward looking statements here or on any of our sales material are intended to express our opinion of earnings potential. Many factors will be important in determining your actual results and no guarantees are made that you will achieve results similar to ours or anybody else's, in fact no guarantees are made that you will achieve any results from our ideas and techniques.

Results vary, and as with any money-making opportunity, you could make more or less. Success in any money-making opportunity is a result of hard work, time and a variety of other factors. No express or implied guarantees of income are made by Fiverr: thirty-five different services for you to sell on Fiverr'

Copyright Fiverr: thirty-five different services for you to sell on Fiverr'

All rights reserved. Unauthorized duplication or publication of any materials from this Site is expressly prohibited.

Introduction

The Fiverr platform is getting more competitive than at any time in recent memory. With top Sellers ruling the site, it can be really hard for anyone who is looking to earn a decent amount of money to succeed. In this book, I'm going to show you thirty-five different Fiverr services that you can do yourself and which will convert like hot cakes.

Now, before we start, these are ideas for gigs. I'm not saying they're going to be suitable for every one of you. Some may not be suited to your abilities, or skill set, although by and large, most of you that are computer literate should be comfortable with the majority of these methods.

The services illustrated will give beginner's an opportunity to begin making cash with Fiverr and it will likewise offer those hoping to take their Fiverr business to the next level, some additional ideas and indeed revenue. That is, if you take action to complete and publish the services.

You can make some cash marketing individuals' businesses, online journals, sites and social profiles utilizing flyers, standard promotions and connections. It's easy to do and for the most part, very simple to provide

To offer your own unique services you need to think of what services you can offer to people that will be of value to them. For instance you could send out diagrams of guitar chords to people who are just learning to play the guitar to help them. It really is that simple.

If you can find a problem that people have and then help them fix that problem, then you can become very successful on the Fiverr platform and In return, make a bucket load of money.

Additionally, whenever you deliver services on Fiverr, or any other freelancing platform, customer service is the name of the game. Get that right and you'll be a winner! Reply to any emails you get from Customers as quickly as possible, always be polite and courteous and remember to leave a great review for your buyer.

Try, If possible, to over-deliver on what you have offered in your description. For instance, If You were to offer Logos, deliver more than you promised, or maybe, you could deliver their order much faster than promised.

The Customers who are amazed by the level of service you deliver could well become repeat customers of the future. Remember, there is no greater advertising than word of mouth. If a Customer recommends you to their contacts your gig could be snowballing to even higher sales

With the introduction of Fiverr packages for use with gigs, sellers are no longer restricted to just getting $5 for sales on the platform , with popular packages also at $25 and $125 this really can be a great money-spinner.

Contents

Fiverr: thirty-five different services for you to sell on Fiverr' 2
Introduction 9
How this book is structured 16
Analysis Paralysis 18
1. Flyers. 22
2. Product Mock-ups 24
3. Links. 26
4. Logo Design 28
5. Designing Banner Ads 32
6. Cartoons 34
7. Social Media design 36
8. Sales Copywriting 38
9. Video introductions 42
10. Workout guides 44
11. Dietary guides 44
12. Online courses 46
13. Presentations 48
14. Voiceovers 50
15. Video Ambassador 52
16. WordPress 53
17. Write on a part of your body 56
18. Email swipes 56
19. Linked-in profile 58
20. Resume writing 62

21. Puppetry 64

22. Celebrity Impersonating 67

23. Spells 69

24. Unusual messages 70

    25. Become someone's friend 74

26. Business advice 76

27. Fake Boyfriend/ Girlfriend 78

28. Researching 78

29. Background removal from photos 80

30. EBook covers 82

31. Business Card Design 86

32. Singing 90

33. Virtual Assistant 91

34. Photo Restoration / editing 92

35. Send a Glitter Bomb 94

Amendment requests on Fiverr. 96

The best way to get orders for your gig is to get a higher ranking in the Fiverr search results 98

Using the Fiverr sales analytics tools 102

Alternatives to selling on Fiverr 104

How this book is structured

In each of the services we look at in this book, we will look at several things: the first is the Fiverr offer idea, secondly what you will need to complete the gig and finally we'll look at volumes of work you can expect (If successful) and also the potential amount of money you could expect to get if you had a top-selling gig in a particular niche. Many people think of Fiverr as a way of earning a few extra bucks, but to some, they earn more than most people could ever expect to earn in their lifetimes.

For you information, there is an accompanying course that goes with this book, which goes into much more detail on how to set-up your account,

How to optimise your title headings, offer description and on-page SEO, as well as how to increase sales and conversions of your customers once you have started your business on Fiverr.

You can get the course, and many other courses, at a discount, by going to:

www.onlinecoursediscounts.com

You will also find you can get some great free stuff there by signing-up for my mailing list.

Analysis Paralysis

Have you ever heard of this phrase? Have you taken courses about making money online and/or read and read and then read some more about Fiverr but still not done anything with the Information that you've imbibed ? This is known as Analysis Paralysis where you've taken in so much Information that you think you'll never be able to do it all.

How much have you actually done to work towards your goal of becoming a Fiverr Seller? Have you done anything at all apart from learn, learn and learn some more. Almost all of those that start out learning about Fiverr never actually follow through by doing anything and therefore are guaranteed to fail. How much have you spent on gaining your education?

To achieve on Fiverr (or any other walk of life) you need to move from the planning or research stage to actually doing something.

Procrastination is the biggest killer of dreams and goals. To combat this, start changing that today. Do something, anything to turn your dream into a reality.

Don't allow yourself to become part of the majority of people who fail just because they don't move past the planning stage.

I'll give you an example of this. Before last July, I wanted to write books and make online courses. I wrote a complete book and built two online courses, but didn't publish them. One day, my Wife said to me "you know what your problem is with so many things in your life? You're a perfectionist and a worrier and you spend so much time doing those two things that you struggle to finish anything at all."

Of course, she was right, the work was done and I had wasted far too much time altering already finished projects. Today I have published over thirty online courses and this is my third book.

So, to get you started, make a website, put up an advertisement (even if it's just on Craigslist) offering links to your Fiverr Gig (landing page.)

It may surprise you how quickly you can profit from these actions, particularly when you combine them with offering some of the ideas in this book.

So, without further ado, let's get on and take a look at the Ideas which, if you do properly, may give you a chance of making some excellent returns on your Fiverr Income.

Now remember, if you don't take action on these, you definitely will not achieve anything. All of the ideas in the book are making money for people on Fiverr. If they can do it, why can't you?

1. Flyers.

Flyers are the leaflets you get handed whilst out shopping. You can also see them in Store Windows, on notice boards and even delivered with the mail. They're primarily a form of advertising, either for a new launch of a product, book or course. Alternatively, they may be advertising a local event, concert, nightclub, open day etc.

They are usually printed on glossy paper and can be folded into a booklet format. So for this service, you offer to hand out 50 flyers (supplied by your Customer) to individuals in your school, college, University, place of work, or at an event/ occasion like a concert, festival etc.

You may have to get permission from local authorities and your government to do this,

so please check with them before offering this service. In some areas you will have to pay a fee for a licence. Please ensure you follow all the local rules and regulations. If you don't, you may well be faced with a hefty fine.

As a gig extra you can offer to get flyers printed or to get the gig done extra quickly. You could even offer a discount for delivering extra multiples of flyers. You will find that very often, customers ordering this service will order up to ten orders at once.

2. Product Mock-ups

According to Wikipedia 'A product mock-up is a scale or full-sized replica of a design, or device used for teaching, demonstration, design evaluation, promotion and other purposes.

People are often after a product mock-up showing their website, app or logo on a variety of things like iPhones, iPads, PCs etc.

If you head over to www.frame.lab25.co.uk you can make product Mock-ups completely free of charge. It takes just a few minutes to do and the finished product is free for both personal and commercial use.

Another site offering free mock up software is mockupworld.co. This is specifically for people with access and knowledge of using Photoshop and provides a whole heap of options including fashion bag, cap, paper bag, invitations and loads more.

There's quite a lot of demand for this product on Fiverr and it can be sold for approximately $20 with service extras

3. Links.

Backlinks are links from one website to another. These are used by search engines like Google to help analyse the importance of the said site. People are willing to buy backlinks from sites in their particular Niche (category) i.e. weight loss, health, make money online etc. Getting links which help boost the position of sites on the search engines is known as getting 'link juice.' There is a whole Industry built from performing this task and it all fills under the heading of 'SEO.'

You can include relevant back links from your online sites to other websites for $5. I see this all the time on Fiverr and they generally appear to make a couple of hundred dollars with this type of gig. Since it runs out after a few months, you can get a considerable measure of resales and develop a decent customer portfolio over a period of time.

All you need to do is ask them to provide you with a short article or banner ad to link to their site. You can charge extra by doing it yourself.

As I mentioned earlier, offering something like this is about the niche your online site is in. I prescribe health, dating, dietary products, sport and news for individuals searching for high benefit sites to set up to offer connections on.

The top-selling gigs in this link building category have over twenty thousand sales each. With prices from $5-$140 for each gig. This makes this opportunity worth a cool $100,000 to well over $2 million if you can do it. That's fantastic money which would change your life forever

4. Logo Design

A logo is designed for company branding and is the graphic you see at the top of their letterheads and compliment slips, as well as on business cards, on advertising and even on company giveaways, as well as some company vehicles.

Logo design is one of the best gigs to offer on Fiverr. If you're great at it, then it's simple to get the designs made for those that want them. Somebody who's experienced at Photoshop can make logos in virtually no time at all. Once you get proficient at this skill, then you'll know how easy and simple it is for them to make 50 + logos inside of 4 hours. I've seen people who can churn out three Fiverr logos in minutes.

The simpler is better.

Think for instance of the eBay logo which is essentially their name spelt out in coloured letters. Other famous logos include the iconic Golden Arches that make up the McDonald's logo and the apple with a bite taken from it which makes up the Apple logo.

Other notable examples include the Nike 'swoosh', the old style writing of 'Ford,' displayed on a blue oval shape, the bright red writing of Coca-Cola, the red tag on Levi's Jeans and the three spokes in a circle which makes up the Mercedes logo.

These are the designs which help us identity with the brands and products. It would be weird getting a coffee from Starbucks without seeing their green logo on the side of the cups. We come to associate the logo with a certain standard of quality.

It will may require investment to get started, yet the real logo platforms shouldn't take you longer than two weeks to learn, and can be even quicker through participating in some YouTube instructional exercises. The top/selling logo makers on Fiverr are earning six figure sums with never ending hoards of customers queued for up to a month waiting for their logo designs. Once you have built up a customer list you can charge extras just for allowing VIP customers to queue jump

So let's take a look at some potential earnings. The top-selling gigs in the logo design category have over thirty-five thousand sales.

With their category prices ranging from $5-$205, for each gig this makes this opportunity worth a cool $175,000 to over $7 million! Isn't that worth learning logo design for?

As I previously mentioned, you can easily take a cheap course on Udemy.com or learn the skills from YouTube to start your logo design gigs.

5. Designing Banner Ads

A banner ad is a form of advertising deliver by an ad server and displayed on the Internet, or World Wide Web (hence the www. On most Websites)

Banner advertisements are something I regularly purchase off of Fiverr. I've noticed the quality of Banner Ad on Fiverr to be higher than when I use other platforms like freelancer that charge $30 +.When you provide good banners ads on Fiverr you will get lots of repeat business and on the off chance that you combine it with logo design you'll be offering two of the best-selling gigs on Fiverr

If you have a website of your own, then you can offer promoting space from $5 (more for larger spaces) you can even make a promoting page where you'll host heaps of various advertisements a year, for the cost of $5 per slot. This is a straightforward yet viable method for getting several hundred dollars each year for doing next to nothing.

Another idea is to create animated banner ads. Although this sounds complicated it can be achieved very quickly and easily through creating a GIF (which means Graphics Interchange Format)

This is just a fancy name for a flashing or blinking graphic and can be done by going to gif maker.me or gifcreator.me and following the very simple instructions on their site. Basically, all it entails is creating two or more images/ texts which their software will scroll through creating the moving image effect. It's very simple to do, but can make you a fair amount of money on Fiverr.

6. Cartoons

This idea is entitled 'Cartoons' but by cartoon I don't mean the traditional Tom and Jerry style cartoon. Maybe this idea would be better suited I'd it were called 'Caricature' but, we'll use cartoon as it's easier.

If you're good at drawing then you could do Cartoons of people. Most people love seeing themselves, or their loved one characterised

In fact, you can learn to draw cartoons fairly easily. I recently watched a TEDX lecture on YouTube, in which the Instructor taught the Audience to draw cartoons of people in just a few minutes. If they can learn it, you can.

There's also software out there where you can Import someone's photo and the software creates a Cartoon from the photograph. So one way or another, it's a great opportunity to make money from your skills.

People love anything like that, despite the fact that it's not as prominent as logo and banner ads it's still worth attempting.

You'll typically get higher priced orders ($25 and above) while offering services for something like this. This is achieved by offering to do the cartoon in colour, extra-large, with multiple characters or extra fast.

7. Social Media design

Social media is all around us.

People spend large amounts of their days on Facebook, Twitter, Pinterest, Instagram, YouTube and the like.

How many people profiles have you visited to see they have stunning graphics in their page headers or on their blog posts. What you probably didn't know is there are people making large amounts of money, offering to build these graphics on Fiverr.

In fact, Social media design is something else I often purchase. I purchase plans for my Twitter and Facebook page, once in a while, and also for YouTube.

If you're great at Social Media Design then these are the gigs for you. When coupled with the right software (and I recommend Canva.com and also Adobe Post) you'll figure out how to become amazingly speedy and effective at making these gigs.

Once you're experienced you can come up with a finished design in just 2-3 minutes. That makes it considerably easier to finish the order and get the cash come flowing in.

You could offer a package for branding all of someone's social media platforms with the same design. This will make you at least $25 per gig.

8. Sales Copywriting

Have you ever had at least some experience making up headlines for you blog etc.? These are copy writing skills. Alternatively, do you think you could write sales copy? If you can compose up to 10,000 words every day then making a Fiverr writing gig could be an awesome approach to acquiring a full-time living from Fiverr.

The top selling sales copywriters on Fiverr sell tens of thousands of gigs.

It's not everyone's cup of tea, but, if you start it you'll find your writing speed improves and you'll soon be able to knock out these writing gigs in no time at all.

Individuals are happy to purchase 50 + gigs from somebody who's great at composing and has fast reaction times and good customer service skills. I've worked in the article composing industry and there's heaps of cash to be made, it's one of the main gigs that individuals reliably purchase on an everyday basis. You may even need just 20 great customers to have the capacity to procure a full-time wage from composing articles.

In my time article composing I found that website

admins who make either SEO gigs or mass AdSense/associate web journals would purchase 5 test articles and afterward in the event they liked what you'd written then they'd buy a year's worth of orders for their weblogs, magazines etc.

Purchasers search for well-written, Informative material that is one of a kind and not spun

If you can convey that everyday then you can without much of a stretch make a gig that your Customers will go crazy for.

By providing quality work, your Customers will come rushing back for more. Simply don't get caught in the trap of composing just any 1000 loosely related words for $5. Quality over the amount will get you a strong customer base that continues returning for additional gigs.

9. Video introductions

There is a high demand for video introductions on Fiverr and you can easily offer this type of gig. There are various sites which offer video templates from between $1-$5.

All you do is add your choice of words to the video template and the order is complete ready to sell to your customer.

You can also download whiteboard animation software for less than $50 if you'd like to make this style of video introduction.

This is a particularly good seller at Christmas and other seasonal holidays. Top sellers have sold over 2000+ of this type of offer, and with an average price of $25+ that would equate to $50,000

People need also need videos for products they're selling on eBay, or Amazon, You Tube, or Facebook and other Social Media Channels, their websites and a whole host of other things.

10. Workout guides

Lots of people are health conscious these days, so the health and fitness niche is a great one to focus your attention on. An offer which fits nicely into this category on Fiverr is Workout guides.

All you need to do is to look up some exercises on You Tube and compile all of the details in a general workout guide. If you want you can make you guide look better with Illustrations, you can get them for a Fiver as a buyer on Fiverr.

Your guide should be 3-4 pages long and available in PDF format. Customers will pay good money for them and once prepared you just have to download them when you receive an order. This order can be completed in just a couple of minutes.

11. Dietary guides

A great companion to the workout guides is to offer dietary sheets. There has recently been a glut of different diets such as the Paleo and Atkins diets which have become very popular.

You could also make up sheets for things like smoothie recipes. Again the Information for these diets is easily available over the Internet. You can offer a whole range of dietary plans to cover different diets. It's a great idea to be upsell other products.

12. Online courses

Online courses make a great product to sell on Fiverr. It will take you from a few hours to a few days to produce a course,

But once they are done you can easily offer them on Fiverr as well as re-using your content by putting your course on various educational selling platforms such as Udemy, Skillshare and Amazon

I've found a great App for phone, tablet and PC which I often use to make courses. It's called Adobe Spark. It costs nothing to download it and comes complete with an extensive selection of royalty-free music, icons and photos. There are also a number of themes, colours and fonts to choose from making it ideal for quickly producing courses on.

I myself have made well on the way to two thousand dollars now by making online courses.

Everyone has some knowledge they can teach someone, whether you're a Housewife who can teach others tricks and hints to remove stains to a high powered business Woman, teaching skills in Asset Finance, everybody has something they can teach.

My own Son is currently working on a World of Warcraft Course and believe me, he's an expert!

If you upload your course to You tube you can use their auto captioning tool to give you a printed version of your course which you can then sell as an eBook on Fiverr and in other places too. There are plenty of courses here on Udemy showing exactly how to make a course. I even have one of my own if you look at the bonus lecture at the end.

13. Presentations

Lots of people require presentations for School work, College, University or work purposes. They also need them for courses on places like Skillshare and Udemy.

There is some great software packages out there on which you can build presentations.

Microsoft PowerPoint, Apple's Keynote and Canva's new presentation software all spring to mind.

You could easily offer to make a number of slides for each presentation for just $5. Additionally, you could offer graphics and voiceover extras to increase the amount you earn per order.

14. Voiceovers

One of the most sought after services on Fiverr is for voiceovers. As time goes on, more and more people will want their E books, turned into Audiobooks, as they realise, it can be a great additional revenue stream

Other sources of Customers are Course Makers, Internet Marketers, and Video Intro Makers.

For you, the Seller, It costs hardly anything to create a voiceover. In fact, it is possible to do them using just a set of iPhone earphones with built in mic and then cleaning up the sound using a free software program such as audacity. Practice your speaking skills in the mirror, so you sound clear and confident. It may be worthwhile teaming- up with someone who is already selling video introductions on Fiverr. That way you can cross-promote each other's products and make much more money. Authors are prepared to pay you good money for this service. The minimum charge you should be looking to make on this type of services is $5 per 500 words spoken.

The top-selling gigs in the voiceover category have over twenty-one thousand sales.

With prices from $5-$50 for each gig, this makes this opportunity worth a cool $105,000 to over $1 million if you can replicate it.

I've often been told I have the face for radio.

15. Video Ambassador

If you are confident with your looks, and being in front of the Camera, you can become a Video Ambassador for companies on Fiverr. Yes, they will actually pay you for promoting their products and will often provide scripts for you to recite. You will also find, many course makers on places like Udemy, will be happy for you to present their work for them.

I've been looking at some of the top gigs in this category marked 'Testimonials' and many of them have sold well over 1000 gigs.

The going rate for this type of service is $5 for 75 words with extras increasing the price per sale by up to $100, by offering things like same day service and delivering the video in HD. This is very easy to do as most modern smartphones are equipped with HD filming facilities.

16. WordPress

Installing WordPress and its associated themes is another big money earner on Fiverr. WordPress is one of the most popular ways to build a website in the World.

Many people are also stuck when it comes to either building a website of their own, or installing the multiple WordPress plug-ins and widgets available to them.

For those of you that have already used WordPress for creating their own blogs or sites, it is very easy to replicate this service for others. It takes about ten minutes to install WordPress once somebody has a domain name and hosting and you can make approximately $10 for each extra page ordered. Top sellers have over 1000 successfully completed orders for this type of gig.

You could also offer your customers a short course or e-book on how to install and set-up WordPress for themselves. All you need to do is host it on Udemy.com or have a pdf copy of your eBook available for download. If you're really good at WordPress then you could offer to transfer one site to another, to build WordPress templates or offer also offer to help people whose sites have been hacked, blacklisted or have other security type issues.

The top-selling gigs in this category have over three thousand sales each.

With their prices ranging from between $5-$500 for each gig (depending on how much work is involved.) This makes this opportunity worth an amazing $9,000-$150,000 for top-sellers. There are plenty of free WordPress tutorials on YouTube for those that wish to learn.

17. Write on a part of your body

Yes, you read it correctly! There are lots of people out there making bank on Fiverr from writing/drawing on various parts of their body. I've just seen a gig from a guy who writes messages on his fat belly (his description, not mine). He's sold almost 1000 orders with extras of up to $50 a time. If he got just $20 per order then that's made him a cool $20,000. It's so simple to do and if you're into allowing yourself to take part in this bizarre gig then this could be for you. You could also offer a gig writing company logos on your hand, face, feet etc

.One word of warning, don't use permanent marker on your face, or body, or else you could be offering free advertising to somebody for a very, very long time.

18. Email swipes

Have you ever ordered anything online where you sign-up to an offer and then over the next few days/weeks and months you continue to get emails from that person offering you a whole host of associated products and daily offers?

More often than not, these have been designed by sales professionals and modified to sell the most of any product over a given length of time.

Internet Marketers will pay you handsomely for creating content to put into their auto/responder list, which they can automatically use to send you regular emails. The content is known as email swipes.

But, I'm not a sales professional who knows how to make email swipes I hear you cry. Well that's no problem. Most people selling things online want you to join their email lists and will send you daily emails. Sign-up to several of these and you will start to receive free emails (or email swipe content.)

You can alter these slightly and use them as an offer on Fiverr. All you need to do is tailor them to your Customers requirements and you will have a ready-made service for Internet Marketers to buy.

19. Linked-in profile

Recently, partly in preparation for this course, I've been scouring the top-selling gigs on Fiverr to see what's selling and I came across quite a few gigs offering to write people's profiles on Linked-in for them. Now at first glance, it looks as if this would be a time consuming thing to do for just a Fiverr. The top-sellers offering this gig had thousands of sales, so I gave their gigs a closer inspection. What they are actually offering their customers is a template for filling in a linked-in profile.

All you need to do is look at any all-star rated profile on linked-in (I have one) and just copy the format of their profile and then design a quick template on Microsoft word or Open Office (or any another word document) to send to the customer once they order the gig.

In my case, my profile consists of

Name

Education

Current job role and brief explanation of what I do (i.e. what the company does, and also, my proficiencies such as Marketing and sales etc.)

Previous work experience again highlighting what I did to earn my wage)

Skills and endorsements (just ask your customer to fill in the skills they think they're good at) and when they link with people they will start to get endorsed for the skills on the list (I have thousands of endorsements)

Recommendations (get a colleague or former colleague to complete a short recommendation)

Then ask your customer to join some work related groups as they also appear on the linked-in profile and voila, you have a completed template (although obviously you will need to flesh it out a bit).

The top-selling gigs in this category have almost ten thousand sales. With prices from between $35-$120 for each gig. This makes this opportunity worth a cool $350,000 to $1,200,000 if you can replicate it. This is a life changing amount of money from one gig.

20. Resume writing

Think of the amount of people who are applying for jobs?

At any one time there could be millions. All of them need to supply their curriculum Vitae (CV) or resume. This is good news for you as it means there's an opportunity to generate some profits.

You can use the linked-in method to offer a resume writing gig. In fact, there are free CV or resume writing templates readily available on the Internet. Customers on Fiverr will pay good money for this service and once again, all you have to do is to provide a template.

Of course, you can also offer to complete the resume, profile or CV for them, but this is offered as a gig extra of between $20- $50. Another useful extra for this type of gig is to order the express delivery within 24 hours gig for which you should be charging at least $20 as people who require resumes often require them quickly.

Another useful extra to offer is giving them the option to have their resume printed and sent to them on good quality paper (only offer this if you have access to both a printer and good quality paper)

The money-making opportunities for this gig are massive for those with the right skills and talent.

21. Puppetry

Believe it, or not, this is a really great-selling gig on Fiverr!

If you have a sense of humour and access to a hand puppet then you could be one of the people selling hundreds of this type of gig on Fiverr. There is a ventriloquist puppet character (Dr .Hans Van Puppet) on Fiverr who talks with a German accent.

He claims in the promo video for one of his gigs to have sold over eight thousand gigs. His package cost for working on any project is now $100. If he was able to make another 5000 sales going forward, his sales would be $500,000. Not bad for a puppet? And the great news is you can do the same!

All you need to do is to get the puppet to repeat the words your customer wants. Yes, they provide the script and if they don't want to, you can charge them another $25-$100 for you to provide one in their behalf.

You don't even have to worry about learning ventriloquism skills, as you do not appear on the screen with the puppet. Use your smart phone to film your gig. You can get free editing software by typing the phrase 'free editing software' into your online search engine.

I've heard a product called 'Screencast-o-matic' is very good, although I've never used it myself. My preferred choice is Camtasia which is available on a free trial.

Many of the puppetry gigs I've seen on Fiverr make up to $100 a time. Ideal ways to offer your puppetry gig for are special occasions like Birthdays, thanksgiving and Christmas.

22. Celebrity Impersonating

Do you look or sound like a famous celebrity? If so, you are very lucky, as there are thousands of buyers on Fiverr for your type of product and a wide variety of lookalikes / sounds likes offering this type of gig. Looking down the list, you will see a long list of 'famous people,' with lots stars of stage, TV and films, sports personalities and the like.

In fact, there is even someone impersonating Barrack Obama who has made hundreds of sales. The list continues with lookalikes of Jesus, Donald Trump, Bill Clinton, Harry Potter, The Muppets, Optimus prime etc.

In fact, there are fans of most celebrities who would buy a short video message from their favourite superstar. Your only limit is your imagination with this gig.

The best-selling gigs in this niche have sold almost one thousand gigs each. With prices starting at $5 for each gig. This makes this opportunity worth $4-5000.

Nice money from a voice that doesn't belong to you. If you can do more than one voice you can multiply your earnings several times over.

23. Spells

I came across this little beauty of a gig recently. People are ordering hundreds of these gigs and so there are lots of money-making opportunities with this one.

There are gigs offering spells to improve your career, make someone fall in love with you and protect you.

Now I'm not saying these types of gigs are for everyone, or making any comment on the validity of whether spells actually work or not, but, people are buying these gigs by the bucket load.

But, I'm no Witch or Warlock I hear you exclaim!

The good news is Spells can be found by searching for them on the Internet and also in old books or spiritual/ fate, mystic or fortune type magazines.

24. Unusual messages

Do you live near to the Beach? You can use the free resources available there to make money on Fiverr.

There are people selling hundreds of gigs just for writing someone's name or company name or logo, in the sand. It literally takes just a few minutes to do and film on your camera phone and you can do several gigs in one visit. You can also do the same type of gig with arranging pebbles on.an Sandy beach, or on any other darkened background.

What about if you don't live near to the beach? Well, there are plenty of options. Try writing out the name with more or less any foodstuff you can imagine. Hot Dog Sausages, various vegetables, you name it.

If not I've seen names written in the froth on top of Coffee, in alphabet spaghetti shapes. The list can be pretty much endless.

You can carve into wood, cut into a lawn using a lawnmower, or write on the steam on a misty window. There are massive opportunities here.

Alternatives, for this type of gig could be using chalkboard or whiteboards to write the name or logos.

The top-selling gigs in this category have over one thousand sales each. With prices from between $5-$20 for each gig. This makes this opportunity worth a wonderful $5,000 to $20,000 if you can replicate it. You can make great money from a fairly simple gig.

25. Become someone's friend.

There are thousands of lonely people out there who need companions, or just someone to talk to. Even people in relationships can feel lonely and cut-off sometimes. They may have relationship or School problems, be insecure about something, or just feeling down and in need of a virtual hug.

This has fostered a tonne of gigs in response on Fiverr and also creates a great opportunity for you, as well as allowing you to make their lives better for them too.

All you need to do is to offer a five minute chat with you on Skype, to be their friend, listen to their problems, give advice or feed-back or just keep them company.

You can also offer a gig extra of additional time with you at a small discount for the longer they order your gig. This gig could earn $40-$50 per hour for those in demand. Think of the things you could buy with that!

26. Business advice

There are hundreds of millions of companies in the World. All of them have to start from nothing and grow through experience, or mentoring. Every time someone has a problem there is money to be made by providing a solution. This is another great chance for you!

Have you started your own business or been in a Senior Management position? There are lots of people out there looking for business advice and there are many ways you can make a gig from the skills you possess.

Every business from start-ups to well-established businesses sometimes need advice and this really is a golden opportunity to make some fast cash.

For instance, you could offer a template for those looking to use it for crowd-funding , a template for starting your own business, a short business consultant Skype chat, a business plan template and the list goes on and on.

Maybe you have financial or operational expertise and can offer advice or guidance? If so, this gig can be a multi-seller for you

27. Fake Boyfriend/ Girlfriend

How many times have you wanted to make someone jealous or get back at them for something they've done? You're not alone. There are loads of people out there who've experienced exactly the same feelings as you. Now, as you've seen in the previous gig ideas; where there's a problem there's money to be made.

You could offer to be someone's fake girlfriend or boyfriend and leave flirty messages on Social Media for them. I've checked the gigs out and yes, people are buying this type of gig. This is Ideal for someone looking for a status boost. Although I'm not condoning this gig, it does make money on Fiverr.

28. Researching

There are a whole host of gigs on Fiverr offering researching for businesses. Different gigs you could offer are to search yellow pages for business leads, researching a product or market, looking for email addresses as sales leads, research for a project or school work, data mining, email scraping, looking for keywords or profitable niches, looking for products to sell on eBay or Amazon and the list goes on and on.

There are people on Fiverr making tens of thousands of Dollars offering this type of gig.

I've taken a look at some of the top gigs for you.

The top gig in keyword research has sold over 1500 gigs and has current package offers up to $15. This gig alone could be worth over $10,000 to them or indeed you

29. Background removal from photos

Have you ever looked at a photo of yourself or someone you know and thought I love the photo, but hate the background (maybe there's someone in it you don't want there or something distracting.) Well, you are not alone. Therefore, there's quite a high demand to have the backgrounds removed from photos. Now the really good news is there is free software available to do this. All you have to do is search for it online and then you can offer this service to people on Fiverr.

Top selling gigs similar to this are selling over 1000+ gigs. With good gig extras you could easily average $15 per gig which makes this gig worth a cool $15,000 or more.

30. EBook covers

According to digitalbookworld.com there are over 125 million e books in the World and almost 50 million audiobooks. Also Google have noted there are over 129 million books published to date. Many of them have several different editions. With the markets growing by 14-40% depending on whose Stats you believe, this is a market which is growing massively year-on-year.

Obviously, not all of those books, e books and audiobooks will make number one in the charts and many won't sell any copies at all.

However, one thing they all need before publishing is a cover.

Therefore, this is one of the most sought after gigs on Fiver. Top sellers of this type of gig have sold twenty thousand plus gigs and with so many books being produced there's plenty of work to go around. It's really easy to do with a little practice. Check out other e book cover designers gigs and see how their book covers look. You will find different genres have different font types and colors.

To start selling this type of gig is really easy and all you need to do is download free e book cover software such as Canva and start practicing.

You can get free images to put on the covers from Pixabay.com, or morguefile.com

With this gig now covered by the new Fiverr packages option, all of your customers will be purchasing either five, twenty-five and one hundred dollar packages for their book covers.

Because of the competition within the e book industry and the need to get high-quality book covers, more will plump for the higher cost options meaning you should easily average twenty-five dollar per gig. That means if you were to become a top seller this gig would be worth a staggering one million dollars plus.

The great thing about this gig is, you can also offer further complimentary services, as both Create space (paperback) and ACX (audiobooks) require different sized book covers than Kindle. You can either offer this as a totally different service, or as gig extras on your original Kindle gig.

Once you're established you may find you have a lot of orders in the queue awaiting completion. Once this happens, offer a gig extra allowing Customers to 'queue jump' in return for an additional payment. I'd suggest a minimum of twenty-five dollars for this concession.

There are a number of other, related services you can offer to go with this gig, including editing (all you need is to get a subscription to grammarly.com, or other editing software, to offer this service.

Formatting can be done on Microsoft word or the free software OpenOffice.org.

You can learn formatting simply by watching one of the many YouTube videos available on the subject and a bit of practice.

The top-selling gigs in the e book category have over fifteen thousand sales each. With prices from between $5-$120 for each gig. This makes this opportunity worth a cool $45,000 to $1,800,000 if you have an artistic eye and can design e book covers.

31. Business Card Design

Business cards are the little cards business people press into your hands when meeting them. It's their way of advertising their business and giving you their contact details all-in-one.

Most businesses need Business Cards for their employees. People like Sales staff, Company Directors and Senior Management regularly hand these out on commercial visits, exhibitions, networking events and in letters etc. You can also use Canva.com for designing business cards. Just simply choose the template from the menu and use one of the free layouts to start with. I would suggest you keep Business Cards fairly simple in their design. The things to include on each business card would be:

Picture of the service offered, or, logo.

Business or person's name

Telephone number

Email address

Address (optional)

Type of service offered

If your Customer has a logo you can offer to put that on their Business Cards as a gig extra. Logos can be imported onto Canva.com so that your design is kept in one place. Once finished, you can download the design as either an image or pdf file.

The top-selling gigs in this category have over three thousand sales each. With prices from between $10-$40 for each gig. This makes this opportunity worth a cool $30,000 to $120,000 if you can replicate it. Nice money from a fairly simple gig.

32. Singing

If you don't mind singing you can offer to sing Happy Birthday for a fiver. From what I've heard, not everyone on Fiverr had the greatest of singing voices, but that can be part of the appeal, getting someone to sing a song, not completely in tune.

Some people wear a fancy dress costume to sing and the gigs seem to be selling very well. Now, I'm not suggesting you copy this, but there's guys on Fiverr singing happy birthday in a thong who've sold over 500 gigs , they're also offering to sing different songs, add a picture in the background , balloons, and extra fast delivery as gig extras.

At an average of $15 this gig is worth a cool $7500. Woman can also get in on the act wearing various fancy dress costumes (and probably make even more than the men.)

33. Virtual Assistant

People are looking for Virtual Assistants to do the mundane online tasks they don't want to do themselves. Virtual Assistants do things like sorting out review swaps for Kindle Books.

This means they will read somebody else's book and leave a review, in return for that person reading your book and leaving a review, and so boosting your ranking in the Kindle Store. This practice should not be confused with buying reviews which is banned by Kindle. A Virtual Assistant can also do things offering Customer Service for a 24/7 website.

Therefore, Offer your services on Fiverr to do things like Data Entry, email research, pdf to Excel, listing things on Amazon or eBay, re-type scanned files etc., as well as the things mentioned above.

You can offer a gig extra of same day delivery and make up to $50 per day with this type of gig.

34. Photo Restoration / editing

This is another great opportunity for you to try on Fiverr.com.

There are a whole host of Apps and programs out there (including Photoshop) which will enable you to make good damage to old photos. You can edit out old scratches, repair tears, add color, enhance the images, get rid of red eye etc. It's even possible with today's software to replace some missing parts of photos

.Many people are willing to pay good money to have their photos restored. Some gigs on Fiverr have sold over one thousand times at an average of $10 each that makes this gig worth up to a cool $10

35. Send a Glitter Bomb

Here's one I found on Fiverr. How often have you really badly wanted to prank someone? Maybe you have a friend, relative, or somebody with something special to celebrate? Somebody who wronged you? Somebody who was nasty? Somebody who turned you down or maybe someone who just deserved it because …..? Well, you're not alone and it turns out lots of people are willing to pay someone to do it for them!

So, where do we come in? We, my friends, are going to assist with a prank and charge for it on Fiverr.

It's simple to do and involves posting an envelope full of glitter to the person of your Customer's choice. With multiple gig extras you could add into this such as birthday/wedding confetti and all sorts of other things, this really could make the money flow in. Top selling gigs in this niche have made over $5000. Not bad for a cheap prank gig.

So there you have it, thirty five different gigs that you can replicate and use to make thousands of dollars on the Fiverr platform. Remember to use all of the available gigs for you to increase your sales level on Fiverr. As a level two seller and above, you're entitled to put up to 20 gigs on Fiverr. The more gigs you put up, the more money you'll make.

Amendment requests on Fiverr.

One thing I come across regularly on the Fiverr Forums is Fiverr sellers complaining about having to offer multiple amendments to the gig they have sent to their customers. For example: someone who has produced a logo being asked to send numerous amendments to the design of the logo.

Now, whilst we should remember that according to sales 'tradition' the customer is always right, that does not mean that you can afford to spend several hours, or even all day working on one five dollar gig. It should also be remembered that some customers are using your gig to re-sell to their customers, so it may be in their interests to get ten versions of that logo, voiceover, or, video you just made. The way around this is to put into your gig description 'if my work was not exactly to your requirement I offer the first two amendments free, after which further amendments require purchase of another gig.'

The best way to get orders for your gig is to get a higher ranking in the Fiverr search results

Here is what I learned from becoming a level 2 seller

1. Use your main keyword in your title and also twice in the gig description.

2. Start your gig description with your main keyword.

3. Add a good quality video to your gig. If you're unable to do it, get a high rated seller on Fiverr to do it (level 2 or TRS).

4. Add a colourful gig gallery picture

5. Mention the name 'Fiverr' in your gig description.

E.g. if you are offering logo design on fiverr, then it would be:"Exclusive Logo Design Gig Only on Fiverr". This trick worked great for me to rank higher on fiverr search results.

6. Offer a no-quibble money back guarantee. This will give your customer the confidence to buy.

7. Use the appropriate tags for your gig. You have several to use. Make sure you use them wisely. Use Google AdWords Keyword Planner to give you good choices.

8. Use a call to action at the bottom of your gig description, such as 'buy it now'.

9. Be patient if you don't get immediate success. Don't give up on selling your gig services in Fiverr. Wait for your time to receive your first order. It will happen!

10. Visit your Fiverr account frequently. You need to visit your account at least every day to stay active. Buyers don't order inactive gig services.

11. Try to sell Private Label Rights products. (PLR) If you don't have the necessary skills to offer in Fiverr, you should try to buy and compile PLR articles and eBooks. You can upload them to your file hosting account, and when someone orders from you, just give your download link

Using the Fiverr sales analytics tools

Fiverr has a great sales aid called Fiverr analytics. It's important you look at this every day

Right at the top of your navigation menu beside your name is a small arrow. Click on the arrow then click your sales, and from the right side, click "Analytics". Take a look at your views or impressions, gig clicks and your CTR, or click though ratio.

Examine your analytics and you will probably see the bounce rate of your gigs or the customers that are viewing your gig and clicking away and at what stage.

From that information, you can learn how to improve the description of your gigs to attract more buyers.

You will be able to figure out the reasons why you have a high bounce rate and low gig conversion and change your gig/s accordingly.

I often try changing both the title and gig gallery picture to try to improve the number of visitors coming to my gigs and Fiverr analytics is an invaluable tool for assisting me in doing this.

Alternatives to selling on Fiverr

There are a large number of different alternatives to selling on Fiverr. You could put your gigs on multiple platforms to multiply your chances of success.

Zeerk.

If you want to sell for a larger price range, maybe you could try Zeerk. From $5 up to 100 dollars, you can offer services, or get a job from a buyer's request.

Gigbucks.

This is one of the biggest and most popular alternatives to Fiverr. Gigs start at $5 dollars, but, goes all the way up to $50. It operates along the same concept as Fiverr.

SEO Clerks.

SEO clerks offer great and trustworthy products, and start at $1 dollar per gig. The best services they offer are SEO-related, and include things like link building, page optimization, and similar services, so not only can you sell on there, but you can also buy some great gigs to re-sell on Fiverr.

Fiverrup

Very similar to Fiverr.com you can sell your gigs between $5 and $100

Tenbux

The look and feel is almost identical to Fiverr apart from the fact the gigs start at $10. The only drawback is the site gets nowhere near the visitors that Fiverr gets.

Dollar3

This website seems a lot better than fiverr or some of its alternatives for pay-outs. For one, it pays out through both PayPal and AlertPay. The sales multiples here can be $5, and some other multiples of 3; $3, $6, $9, $12, $15, $27, $45, and $90.

I hope this list helps you get even more income. If you google the phrase 'alternatives to Fiverr' you can find another 50 similar type sites.

If you're looking for more Fiverr sales tips, hacks and training don't forget to check out my best-selling Fiverr courses:

Fiverr: How to get amazing Income from Fiverr

https://www.udemy.com/fiverr-gigs-you-can-sell-on-fiverr/?couponCode=FROMTHEBOOK

And, How to get amazing success from Fiverr

https://www.udemy.com/how-to-get-amazing-income-from-fiverr/?couponCode=FROMTHEBOOKTOO

So there you have it, a complete beginner's guide to making money on Fiverr. The most important thing for you to do now is to take action. You will achieve absolutely nothing by procrastinating, worrying about whether your gigs are good enough, or if you've got what it takes to be successful. Like the Nike slogan says 'Just do it!' Before too long, you could have a number of successful gigs up on the Fiverr platform. Lots of people make serious, life-changing amounts of money and there's no reason why you can't be one of those people. At least give it a try. What do you have to lose? You really do have your destiny in your own hands.

www.ingramcontent.com/pod-product-compliance
Lightning Source LLC
Chambersburg PA
CBHW070328190526
45169CB00005B/1796